THE WEAPONS ENCYCLOPÆDIA

TANK AIRCRAFT AFV SHIP ARTILLERY VEHICLES SECRET WEAPON

TWE-004 EN

MEDIUM TANK M13-14-15

THE WEAPONS ENCYCLOPAEDIA

PUBLISHED BY

Luca Cristini Editore (Soldiershop), via Orio, 35/4 - 24050 Zanica (BG) ITALY.

DISTRIBUTION BY

Soldiershop - www.soldiershop.com, Amazon, Ingram Spark, Berliner Zinnfigurem (D), LaFeltrinelli, Mondadori, Libera Editorial (Spain), Google book (eBook), Kobo, (eBoook), Apple Book (eBook).

PUBLISHING'S NOTES

None of unpublished images or text of our book may be reproduced in any format without the expressed written permission of Luca Cristini Editore (already Soldiershop.com) when not indicate as marked with license creative commons 3.0 or 4.0. Luca Cristini Editore has made every reasonable effort to locate, contact and acknowledge rights holders and to correctly apply terms and conditions to Content. Every effort has been made to trace the copyright of all the photographs. If there are unintentional omissions, please contact the publisher in writing at: info@soldiershop.com, who will correct all subsequent editions.

LICENSES COMMONS

This book may utilize part of material marked with license creative commons 3.0 or 4.0 (CC BY 4.0), (CC BY-ND 4.0), (CC BY-SA 4.0) or (CC0 1.0). We give appropriate attribution credit and indicate if change were made in the acknowledgments field. Our WTW books series utilize only fonts licensed under the SIL Open Font License or other free use license.

CONTRIBUTORS OF THIS VOLUME & ACKNOWLEDGEMENTS

We thank the main contributors to this issue: The profiles of the tanks are all by the author. Photo coloring by Anna Cristini. Special thanks to national and/or private institutions such as: Army General Staff, State Archives, Bundesarchiv, Nara, Library of Congress, etc. To P. Crippa, A.Lopez, L.Manes, C.Cucut, Tallillo archives, for making available images or other of their archives. Many thanks to Ollie for correcting the English text.

For a complete list of Soldiershop titles, or for every information please contact us on our website: www.soldiershop.com or www. cristinieditore.com. E-mail: info@soldiershop.com. Keep up to date on Facebook & Twitter: https://www.facebook.com/ soldiershop. publishing

Title: **ITALIAN MEDIUM TANK M13/40, M14/41 & M15/42** Code.: **TWE-004 EN**

Series edited by L. S. Cristini

ISBN code: 978-88-9328775. First edition: September 2022

THE WEAPONS ENCYCLOPAEDIA (SOLDIERSHOP) trademark of Luca Cristini Editore

ITALIAN MEDIUM TANK M13/40, M14/41 & M15/42

LUCA STEFANO CRISTINI

BOOK SERIES FOR MODELERS & COLLECTORS

CONTENTS

▼ Tank M13/40 in Tripoli area, February 1941, belonging to the 132nd Ariete Armoured Division.

INTRODUCTION

It was the Italian medium tank par excellence during World War II, the most widely produced and used by the Royal Army along with the later M14/41 and M15/42 versions. The M13/40 was also the first Italian (armored) tank to represent a real threat against opposing tanks, operating mainly against the British on the North African front. To save time and money, as well as to speed up the development, the M13/40 was conceptually based on the M11/39, but equipped with a completely redesigned upper hull. It had a turret large enough to hold a 47 mm (1.85 in.) Breda Model 35. This was an excellent anti-tank gun with performance (quite) similar to the Russian 45 mm (1.77 inch) gun used in their T-26 and tanks. The firepower was complemented by twin 8-mm Breda machine guns placed in the hull and another 8-mm,(coaxial)*coaxially mounted/ that fired tracer rounds. The enumeration of the tank was a combination given by the capital letter "M," referring to medium, according to the Italian tank weight standards of the time, and the number 13, referring to the expected tons of weight, followed by the year of production, in this case 1940. The same applied to later versions.

THE DEVELOPMENT

It was designed in 1937 by Fiat-Ansaldo, and the following year, 1938, the first prototype was built. Based on the earlier M11/39 tank it differed from it in many respects, mainly in the type and arrangement of armament and the completely revised hull. In the new vehicle the main armament, a 47/32 cannon, was mounted in a horseshoe-shaped revolving turret and not in the hull, a solution that greatly reduced the weapon's effectiveness, as in its predecessor.

▼ M13/40 tank in North Africa, November 1941. The tank crew salutes the war reporter before heading for the battle line with their vehicle.

▲ Tank M14/41 of the 132nd Ariete Armoured Division in North Africa. The vehicle advances in the Cyrenaica sector in January 1941. Note the use of reinforcing the turret with pieces of track and the presence of petrol cans attached to racks on the hull typical of this version.

As a secondary armament, the M13/40 had four 8mm machine guns: one coaxial with the gun, two in casemate (a position attributed to the primary armament in the previous model), and one with an anti-aircraft function mountable on a special mount at the outer top of the turret.
In December 1939 all Italian production of medium tanks concentrated on the M13/40, closing the assembly lines of the now outdated M11/39. In 1941 a new version was made with a different engine, one of the weak points of the first vehicle, called the M14/41, from which was also derived the self-propelled 75/18, Sermovente assault gun also good in the anti tank role (a good tank fighter), considered the best Italian armored vehicle employed during World War II. In 1942 a third and final version called M15/42 was conceived which incorporated improvements from battlefield experience, a rear lengthened by 15 cm and a more powerful gun.An experimental prototype for air transport was also made using a Caproni CA 180 airplane that was able to carry the M13/41 tank stowed below the fuselage.

■ TECHNICAL CHARACTERISTICS

The tank consisted of the chassis or hull, armament, engine and related transmission, drive and control components. It had a mass that varied, depending on the model, between 14 and 15 tons. It was 4.9 to 5.06 meters long, 2.28 meters wide and 2.37 meters high.
It comprised the following main parts: hull - accesses - inspection hatches - drain holes - observation - engine - transmission systems - steering and braking systems - external drive and suspension.

Hull: consisted of special steel plates (forming the armor) rigidly connected on the inside by a strong framework of sections and reinforced by crossbeams, so as to obtain a watertight compartment resistant to the most violent stresses and shocks.
At the bottom, the hull was watertight, a fact that enabled it to ford torrents. The plates constituting the armor have different thicknesses and are distributed in such a way as to ensure maximum protection to

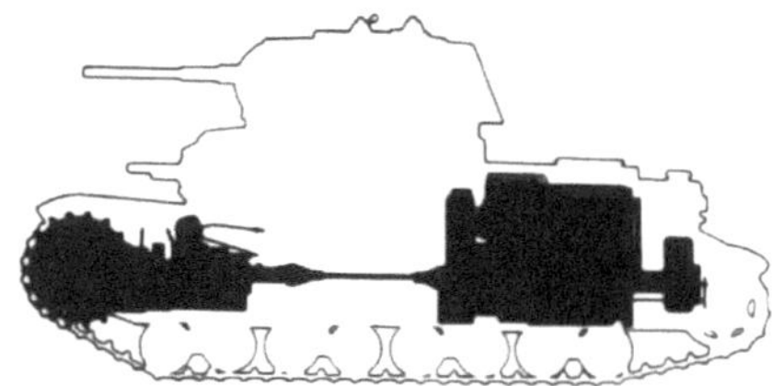

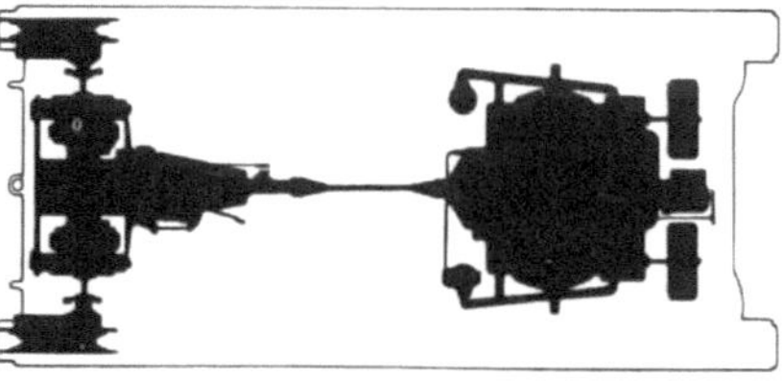

▲ Diagram of the M14/41 tank with description of the engine and transmission.

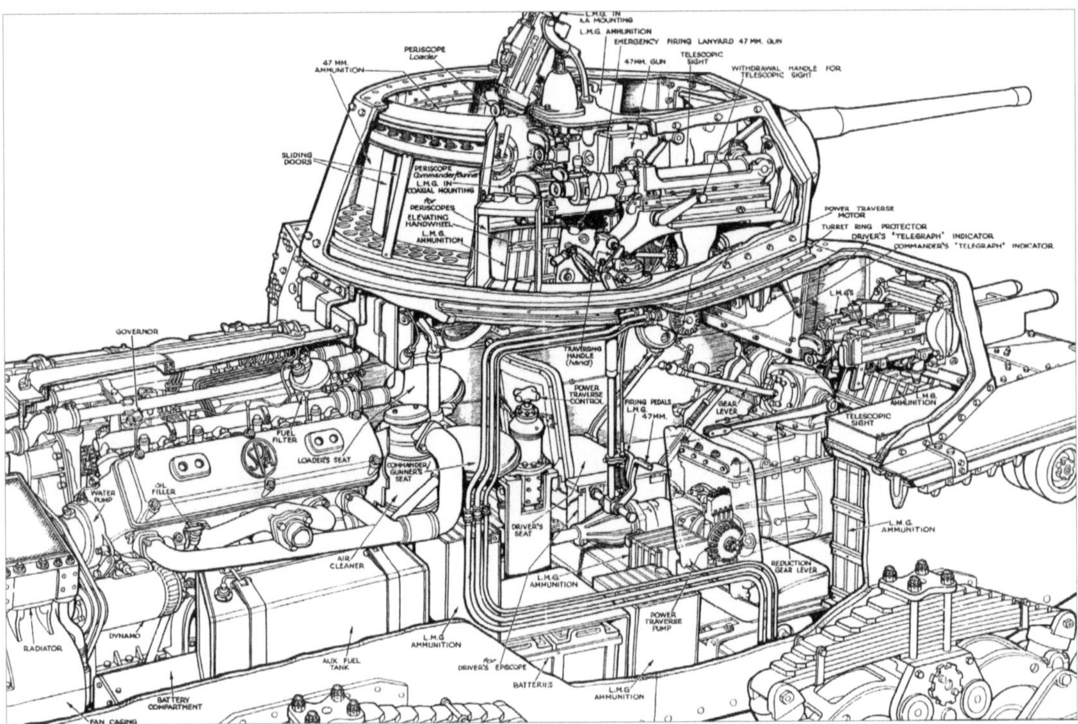

▲ Sketch of the interior of the tank and turret taken from a British study of a captured tank.

the parts most exposed to fire. Inside, the hull is divided into two parts by a vertical bulkhead so as to form an engine space at the rear, and a fighting compartment at the front.

The engine area contains, in addition to the engine with fans and radiators, the two diesel fuel tanks and the storage batteries. The combat area comprises the middle and forward parts of the hull. In it are contained all the tank driving and transmission systems.

In the fighting compartment are located: the crew (4), the ammunition racks and shelves, the radio station and the hull machine guns combination with its range finding scope. The roof has a large circular opening on which the turret supported and a rectangular opening for the observation periscope to pass through.

The turret is mounted on the hull by means of the ring which allows it to rotate 360°. The turret can be turned by hand or by means of the hydraulic apparatus "Calzoni," which consists of a pump, a servomotor and a distributor. The pump is driven by a shaft connected to the transmission shaft.

The turret houses the 47/32 cannon, a coaxial machine gun, a scope elevator and two panoramic scopes. On the turret top is a mount for installing a machine gun for anti-aircraft fire and defense.

Entrances: one on the left side of the hull for the gunner and pilot (right in the M15/42 model); one in the turret for the loader and commander .The port hatch can be kept partially open by means of a stay with a similar arrangement for the two turret hatches.

Inspection hatches: two on the engine chamber and two for the brakes.

The two doors on the engine hood are attached by a central hinge. They are closed from the outside by means of two bolts with wing nuts and from the inside by means of special safety latches.

The two front hatches for inspection of the brakes can be opened only from inside the tank by means of a device controlled by the driver. This makes it possible to keep the hatches partially open during travel for brake cooling.

Means of visibility from inside the tank: for driving, the driver has a rectangular window cut into the front plate, with a hatch hinged on the outside and operated by a lever from the inside. The hatch can assume a fully open position (remaining nearly horizontal) and all other intermediate positions until fully closed.

With the hatch closed, direct visibility is possible through a longitudinal slot, which can be closed from the inside by means of a plate attached to the hatch and operated with a special pin.

The driver's eyes are protected from shrapnel by a thick glass block in a box attached to the plate and easily removable.

In addition to direct visibility, the driver has at his disposal, for driving purposes, a device of indirect visibility consisting of a periscope. This apparatus, which allows the driver to be protected during combat, comprises two prisms, an upper one - objective - protruding from the roof of the hull, and a lower one -ocular- placed in the interior at the driver's eye level. For rear and side visibility, the loader and commander have circular slots in the hull (two on the front plate, one on the right side and one on the driver's access hatch) that can be closed by turning plates operated from the inside. These also allow, in addition to visibility, the use of small arms for close-range defense from inside the tank.

Indirect visibility by the loader and commander is exercised by means of panoramic telescopes. These devices allow 360° vision (they are arranged in the turret through an elastic connection) mounted on a flexible connection/ that dampens vibrations and shocks while on the move. The top of each scope is protected by a special steel guard, from which only the lens projects.

Engine: four stroke, diesel type; 8 cylinders in a block -four on each side- arranged at 90°, V-position. This type of engine differs fundamentally from the normal internal combustion engine in that fueling

▼ Interior of the cockpit-combat chamber.

and ignition are carried out quite differently. The diesel engine and fuel , being much harder to ignite was an innovation and no doubt saved many tank crew lives.

A filter intended to retain any impurities and dust in the air is inserted at the end of the intake duct. The fuel for the cylinders is supplied by special injection pumps, one per cylinder, grouped in a single mechanical complex, controlled by the engine. Ignition of the injected fuel takes place automatically, except for the first cold engine start, which is assisted by spark plugs. After that the normal bursting phase takes place and then the exhaust phase, concluding the operating cycle, which is renewed in full, as in all normal four-stroke internal combustion engines.

Engine starting: 1) *By hand* either from inside or outside the wagon, by means of a crank-operated inertia starter equipped with a clutch button. 2) *Electric*, by means of two starter motors acting on a gear wheel applied to the flywheel.

Lubrication: oil circulation is by means of three pumps, combined in a single body, two of which are scavenge pumps and one is a delivery pump. The scavenge pumps draw oil from the two sumps and send it to the oil tank.

Cooling: is forced water circulation by centrifugal pump. The pump is driven by a double chain and a sprocket inserted on the crankshaft. Water cooling is achieved by fans blowing air through the two radiators.

Air filters: there are four of them, applied to the engine two on each side; they consist of a winding of metal mesh in which a filter of special fabric is housed. Their task is to filter air before it enters the cylinders during the intake phase.

▼ Interior of the cockpit-combat chamber, detail of the turret space.

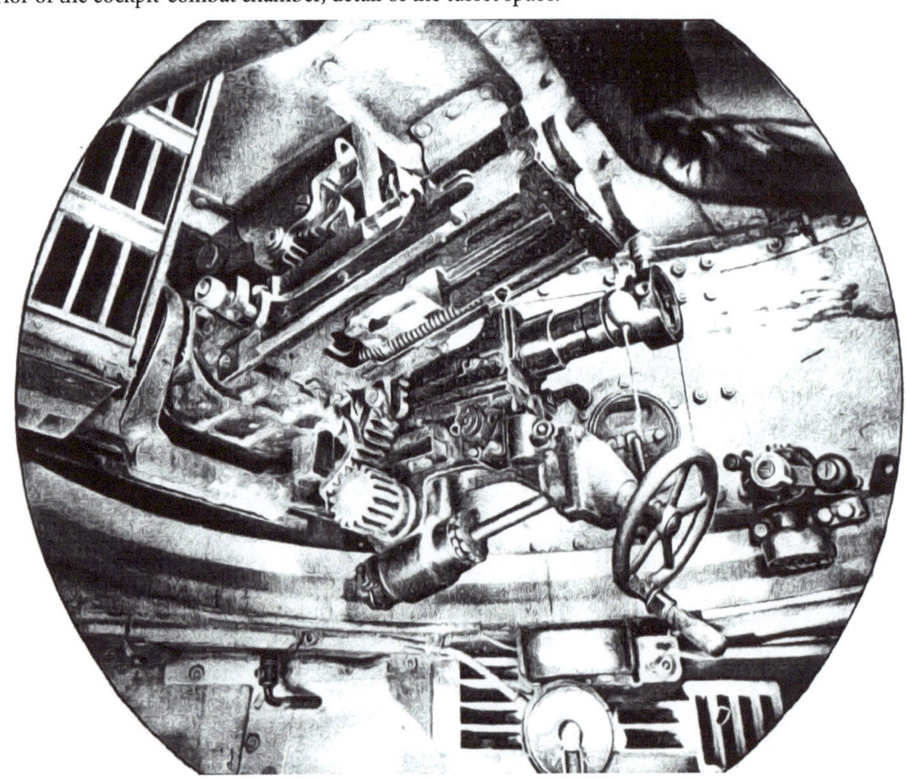

Transmission and clutch systems: incorporated in the engine flywheel, it consists of: a clutch drive housing; a pressure plate ring; a driven plate, set on the clutch shaft and twelve springs. The clutch is released by actuating the pedal controlling the clutch release sleeve, which in turn causes the pressure plate to move away by compressing the springs.

Transmission: the drive shaft is used to transmit the movement of the crankshaft to the gearbox and planetary assembly arranged at the front of the tank. The shaft is protected by a tube and protective cover and is equipped with universal joints.

Gearbox: the gearbox is of the sliding block type, with gears always engaged and direct drive; three shafts: primary, subsidiary, secondary and a reverse gear shaft. In the box, separated by a wall, is the speed reducer, which makes it possible to make a reduction to the normal gears. Therefore there are four normal and four low ratio gears. A lever is used to engage this reduction and directly connect the secondary shaft of the gearbox with the axle, that is, the truncated cone assembly and the epicycle.

Direction and braking systems: they are part of an epicyclic system which is designed to allow the transmission of motion to the wheels, direction and braking. To control the driving of thetank, two direction levers are arranged on the left side of the driver. Maneuvering these levers causes braking of the tracks and consequently steering, which pivots on the braked track.

Brakes: slowing down and stopping is achieved by acting simultaneously on the two direction levers; to have more vigorous braking, the brake pedal is pressed at the same time, which therefore functions exclusively to intensify the braking action.

External propulsion and suspension systems - Drive wheels: these are located on the sides of the hull at the front and receive motion from the drive shafts. They consist of a wheel with two flanges to which are attached two toothed rings for transmitting motion to the track. Also attached to the inner flanges of the wheels are internally toothed sprockets that mesh with the pinions that receive motion from the semi-axles and protrude from the front circular openings of the hull.

Tracks: each track consists of 8 links that are equal to each other and hinged together by pins, the slipping out of which is prevented on the one hand by a stop in the hole in the last hinge and, on the other, by a stop pad embedded in a slot in the links. In the center each link bears a guide flap and, on either side of that flap, two rectangular holes into which the teeth of the driving wheels go.
Idler wheels and idler units: the two tracks, which at the front make use of the drive wheels, rest at the rear on two idler wheels, the pins of which are carried by longitudinally displaceable idler arms. Such displacement causes the track to increase in tension or loosen.

Guide rollers: each track is guided and rests its upper branch on three rubberized rollers, rotating on pins attached to the sides of the hull.

Suspension: through the pins of four plates bolted to the hull sides, the tank rests elastically on four bogies, two on each side. The bogies, each consisting of two pairs of rubberized rollers, are located on the sides of the hull so that the load is evenly distributed on each. Each bogie is independent of the others and has the ability to swing around the pivot of the relevant plate. The flexible system, consisting of springs, levers, and rocker arms that make it up, not only ensures a flexible suspension, but also allows the track to adapt to any unevenness in the terrain and keep in constant contact with the carriage rollers, eliminating one of the main causes of sliding.

Armament: the M13 tank was armed with an Austrian-designed Bhöler Model 35 cannon 47/32 with an initial complement of 87 shells in combat, often increased to almost a 100. The cannon had a depression and elevation of -10° and +20°. To allow greater depression of the weapon on the turret roof there was a removable armor platenin front of the access hatches, which served to increase interior space. The weapon could be operated by a foot pedal or manually. The gun was generally judged favorably, at least in terms of accuracy and reliability. The two Breda 38 machine guns (designed specifically for use on tanks) were positioned in the right front of the hull, in a special ball mount having a firing arc of about 30°, 15° on each side. Another Breda 38 was placed in the turret, co-axially to the gun, on the left side. A fourth Breda 38 was usually available for anti-aircraft use and could be mounted on a special toggle in the center of the turret, just forward of the access hatches. In all, the tank had a normal supply of 2592 8mm caliber cartridges. The Breda 38s had a firing rate of about 450 rounds per minute, a 25-round magazine, and a muzzle velocity of about 792 m/s. In North Africa there were jamming problems due to sand.

Armor: the type of construction and quality of materials used in Italian tanks were not up to the standard of foreign production, especially with regard to the strength of the armor plates. The armor was also bolted on, not cast. The armor often tended to split on impact with an enemy projectile, even if there was no penetration, because it was too "rigid," not very malleable, and poorly treated. The armor reached a maximum thickness of 42mm at the front of the turret and a minimum of 14mm at the bottom of the hull. The sides were protected by only 25mm while the huge left side access hatch was a particularly weak point with only 8mm of armor.

Internal arrangement: engine starting was either electrically or by hand by means of an inertia starter that could be operated both outside and inside the vehicle. The tank was equipped with an electrical

▼ Interior of the cockpit-combat department, detail of the breech piece.

system that provided external lighting (with two lights placed on the sides of the hull and a single light placed in the rear) and internal lighting with two bulbs on the dashboard and two in the fighting compartment. The system obviously also provided engine starting.

The elevation of the gun was controlled by hand by means of a handwheel to the left of the gunner commander while the swing was achieved by rotating the entire turret of the vehicle by means of a handwheel placed to the right of the gunner or by means of a hydraulic system of the "Calzoni" type placed in the center. This system was judged unnecessary and cumbersome so much so that it was very often removed to lighten the tank as it could be useful in mountainous terrain to make the turret move easily in steeply sloping terrain but it was not necessary in the desert terrain of North Africa.
The driver had a hatch window that could remain open while on the move. In combat situations he could take advantage of indirect visibility through a periscope with magnification. Two periscopes were positioned in the turret for observation, again with low magnification.
The gunner in the hull had a telescope positioned between the two machine guns with low magnification. The telescope for the gunner was located on the right side of the turret and was monocular, with a magnification of 1.25x and a horizon sector of 30°. It was graduated for a range of 1200 meters for the cannon and 900 for the machine gun. All optical instruments were built by the San Giorgio company.

Radio system: the radio system, which was almost completely absent in the first tanks produced, consisted of a set of the type "RF1 CA", positioned on the right side of the hull, next to the gunner.
For internal communications, a telegraph, called the *"SD1 internal run indicator"*, was mounted, similar to the telegraph in a ship's engine room, which connected, theoretically, the driver with the commander.

▼ Interior of the cockpit-combat department, detail of the rear near the engine.

The latter could give instructions to the driver by placing a lever on a kind of clock, which automatically appeared in the pilot's view on his "screen"; the disadvantage was that it could be used only when the turret was in the 12 o'clock position (i.e., with the gun facing the direction of travel).

An intercom system was used for three of the crew (minus the driver who used the telegraph) with throat microphones and headsets. Unfortunately, both the commander and the loader in the turret could not use the system if the turret was turned to 6 o'clock (sideways) because the throat microphones were plugged into the lower part of the carriage and had to be disconnected before starting movement.

Source: S.M.R.E. - "*Nozioni di armi, tiro e materiali vari*", Edizioni Le "Forze Armate", Roma, 1942.

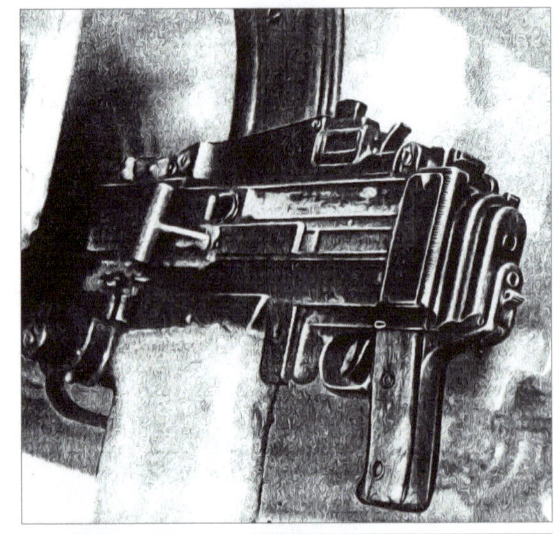

▲ Above: the coaxial machine gun, mounted to the left of the 47 mm cannon on a two-bracket mount carried on the cradle.

In the middle: the two Breda 8 mm. M.G. are mounted on the right side of the front vertical plate in a gimbaled mount with a fixed outer shell and a movable spherical inner shell. The armoured shrouds of the guns are welded to the shell.

◄ View of the tank instrument panel and the open panel for the front view of the vehicle.

VERSIONS OF THE VEHICLES

Three major versions were made of the main medium tank in the Royal Army, including final operatives and prototypes. The most important ones are:

- *M13/40*: first designation of the Ansaldo Medium tank, designed by Fiat-Ansaldo in 1937. The first new model was based on the M11/39 tank. This version was produced in 710 examples. The armament based mainly on the 47/32 mod. 1935 cannon in the turret and Breda mod. 1938 coaxial machine gun, also in the turret, and two other Breda mod. 38s in the hull with a fourth Breda that could be installed on the roof of the turret in an anti-aircraft function.
The M13/40 was powered by a liquid-cooled, 8-cylinder SPA 8T Diesel engine. The associated gearbox counted 4 forward gears and a normal reverse gear; in addition, thanks to the built-in reduction gearbox, 4 more gears plus an additional reverse gear were available. The engine chosen was one of the tank's major handicaps: underpowered and prone to various sand-related failures due to the lack of filters.

- *M14/41:* model produced in 695 examples and equipped with the new 145 hp Fiat SPA 15T V-8 diesel engine. The tank, an evolution of the M13, was almost identical to its predecessor, both in mechanics and armament. The hull differed in the shape for the twin machine guns and in that track guards extended along the entire length of the tank. The new engine also involved new radiator grilles, with fins oriented parallel to the major axis of the tank. A lever for the drive wheel was introduced, that improved traction in mud, and other improvements that affected the electrical system. Also identical was the armament and its arrangement. In addition to the combat tanks, 34 radio command tanks were also produced. Its chassis served as the basis for the 90/53 self-propelled tank and also for the creation of the prototype Saharan Celere Tank.

▲ Final prototype of the M15/42 tank; note the elimination of the access hatch, now placed on the other side.

- *M15/42*: produced in an uncertain number estimated from 112 to 248 units, it was the third and final version and an overall improvement in every respect, but considering the time, it was now an even more inferior vehicle than the original compared to the enemy tanks it would face. Due to the consequent events of the Cassibile armistice of September 3rd, the production was stopped. Moreover, the number of units delivered to the Royal Army was only 82, while the others ended up being used by the Germans and the regular army of the Italian Social Republic. The main differences with the previous versions were: a greater length of the vehicle in the rear by about 15cm; the abolition of the access door on the left side replaced by ammunition racks with the crew access hatch moved to the right side; the exhaust mufflers were better armored; fitted with the new 47/40 gun equipped with a longer barrel and a revamped machine gun position. First prototype dates from March 1943, with official production begun soon after. After September 8, 1943, as mentioned, the Germans took possession of many M15/42s, 92 to be exact, including some command tanks. They then ordered twenty-eight more which were delivered in 1944. The tanks used by the Germans were renamed *Panzerkampfwagen* M15/42 738, all of which were regularly equipped with an RF1 CA radio and immediately distributed to three armored detachments serving in the Regular Army. A small part also was assigned to the *22nd SS-Freiwilligen-Kavallerie-Division "Maria Theresa"*, formed mostly of Hungarian personnel in April 1944. The wreckage of these were seen in Budapest in December 1944 and at least one of the tanks was converted in the field as a recovery vehicle by mounting a crane on the hull.

▲ M13/40 tank transported near Tobruch in June 1942 (State archive).

▲ M15 tank image in anti-aircraft version. The armament consisted of a four barrelled Scotti-Isotta Fraschini 20 mm cannon system, designed in 1932 by engineer Alfredo Scotti, who later sold the patent (but only for foreign countries) to the Swiss company Oerlikon, the weapon was then developed in Italy by Isotta Fraschini in 1938. The Mod.1939 version installed on a stanchion mount was used by the Regia Aeronautica for the defence of installations and by the Regia Marina on board ships and sometimes in (even in) pairs.

▼ M14/41 command tank.

- M.40, M.41 and M.42 command tanks: produced in a total of 139 units, they served mainly to direct the fire of artillery self-propelled vehicles, almost all based on the medium tank hull.

The turret was removed and the roll ring closed with an 8-mm-thick armor plate, in which two hatches were cut; an 8-mm Breda Mod. 38 was mounted on the roof in an anti-aircraft function. Instead, the two Breda Mod. 38s in the hull were replaced by a single 13.2-mm Breda Mod. 31, and two Magneti Marelli radios, one RF1 CA and one RF2 CA, and two extra batteries were placed in the hull; finally, a rangefinder was installed.

-M14/41 Radio Centre: in addition to the standard Magneti Marelli RF1 CA radio, it was equipped with an RF2 CA. The antennas were mounted on the left side of the hull and, by means of a knob, it was possible to lower them from inside the combat chamber to allow rotation of the turret to that side. Thirty-four M14/41CRs were produced, which were distributed at the rate of two vehicles per Battalion command. After the armistice it was used by the Germans and renamed Pz Bef Wg M41 771.

-M15/42 anti-aircraft tank: a very interesting version based on the basic model but equipped with a new polygonal turret obtained by welding, open on the sky, pivoting for 360° and containing a quadruple system of 20 mm Scotti-Isotta-Fraschini 20/70 guns.

The only other change involved the elimination of the two Breda Mod. 38 machine guns in the hull, the opening of which was covered by a 42 mm thick plate. The crew dropped from four to three men, two in the turret and the driver in the hull. Only one prototype (perhaps two) was built, and in early 1943 it was presented and tested at the Army's Center for Motorization Studies. Compared with the original vehicle, the self-propelled anti-aircraft vehicle weighed 14.7 tons, and was taller (2.55 meters). In March it entered service as the "M15/42 Anti-Aircraft Tank" and was given to the 8th Autieri Regiment stationed at Cecchignola in Rome. Here following the armistice the Germans found and captured it. Of its use, the most credited hypothesis has it that the vehicle ended up in Austria where it took part in the fighting and was

▼ Column of M14/41 tanks pass through a Libyan village in 1942. (Archive P. Crippa. Author's colouring).

MEDIUM TANK M13-40 IN NORTH AFRICA

▲ M13/40 belonging to the XXI Battalion, 2nd Company 3rd Squadron of the 132nd Ariete Armoured Division. This vehicle is famous because it was captured along with others from the same division by the British army in the Agedabia area in Libyan Cyrenaica in February 1941.

used until April 1945, where it operated in the Teupitz area, for air defense by the V SS Armored Mountain Corps (*"V-SS Volunteer-Freiwilligen-Gebirgskorps"*) that fought the last battles against the Red Army. Regarding the hypothesis of the two prototypes, it appears that the second would have been transported to Tunisia, where it was tested under real combat conditions. It remained on African soil after the surrender of the Italian 1st Army and 5th *Panzerarmee* in May 1943.

- Semovente versions

Medium tanks, in their main versions, also served as the basis for the development and study of a large series of armored self-propelled vehicles such as the following:

-M.40, M.41, M.42 75/18 self-propelled vehicles: produced in 364 units.

-M.41 da 90/53: produced in only 30 units.

-75/34 M.42: produced in 120 examples under the supervision of the Germans

-Ansaldo 105/25 M.43: produced in 120 units, was used mainly by the Germans.

-Ansaldo 75/34 M.43: produced in 29 units, was used exclusively by the Germans.

-Ansaldo M43 da 75/46: produced in just 11 units, was used exclusively by the Germans.

These specific vehicles will be better covered in subsequent publications on Italian self-propelled vehicles in our series.

▼ Nice close-up of an M14/41 with the tank commander at the turret. Africa 1942. (Archive P. Crippa. Author's colouring). Above: detail of the tank drive wheel.

MEDIUM TANK M13-40 GREECE CAMPAIGN

▲ M13/40 Tank 1 of the 1st Platoon, 1st Company and 4th Battalion of the Centaur Division at Monastir in Gregia - March 1941.

▲ General Mario Balotta in North Africa, Commander of the Ariete Division and winner of the Battle of Bir el Gobi, photographed in 1941 next to an M13/40 tank.

OPERATIONAL USE

Beginning in 1939, the year of its substantial entry into service, the Medium M Tank in all its variants was present in all wartime events involving Italy until 1945.

■ FIRST USE: CAMPAIGN OF GREECE AND ALBANIA

Due to the high production numbers, almost all Italian armored divisions received large quantities of these new medium tanks, which replaced older and obsolete models (I CV3 light tank or even the aging Fiat 3000). The first engagements came with the Albania and Greek campaigns in late 1940.

■ FIRST MAJOR EMPLOYMENT IN NORTH AFRICA

The M13/40 and its successors were then also immediately used in all North African campaigns until 1943. First of course was the M13/40, which by 1941 was joined by its successor the M-14/41. Medium tanks, however, were not used on the Eastern Front, where Italian forces were equipped only with L6/40 tanks and the self-propelled 47/32. Starting in 1942, the Italian Army recognized the weak firepower of the M-series and employed the 75/18 Semovente alongside tanks in its armored units to increase their firepower.

■ THE FIRST WARTIME ACTIONS

The first of more than 700 M13/40s was delivered before the fall of 1940. However, the operation was not well organized, so most of the units were hastily formed and thus lacked cohesion. Another serious problem was that the tanks were not provided with radio equipment, thus making them already poorer performing than their opponents even before combat began.

▼ M13/40 tanks operating in the North African desert circa 1941. Bundesarchiv (author's colouring).

The crews had received almost no training or it was of very limited standard. In 1940 crews spent only 4 weeks of actual tank training and then were immediately sent to the front. The medium tanks' baptism of fire came with a special unit, the **Babini Group**. Arriving too late to fight in the September offensive, this unit was not ready until December 1940 during the British offensive Operation Compass. The tanks of the 3rd Battalion were then present in the Battle of Bardia, where in two days of fighting (Jan. 3-4, 1941) the Australians suffered 456 casualties, while the Italians fared much worse, losing as many as 40,000 men including 2,000 killed, 3,000 wounded and 36,000 captured. During the British offensive, many M13/40s were captured in good condition and later reused. Australian ones later fought particularly at Tobruk, showing large kangaroos painted on the hull and turret (see plate on p. 28).

On February 6 and 7, the British offensive penetrated to such an extent that **Babini Group** tried to turn the British lines present at the Battle of Beda Fomm, in a desperate attempt to allow the cut-off Italian troops to retreat along the Libyan coast. The attack failed and all the tanks were lost. The last six surviving tanks were destroyed shortly thereafter by the British using their 2-pound (40 mm) anti-tank gun tito. Many of these tanks were lost in this campaign to artillery fire rather than other tanks in large part this was due to their relatively poor armor. Some captured M11 and M13 tanks were reused by the Australian 2/6th Cavalry Regiment and the British 6th Royal Tank Regiment, until the spring of 1941, when their fuel ran out and they were subsequently destroyed. Medium tanks also fought in Greece, in difficult terrain, and in April 1941 the M13s of the 132nd Ariete Armored Division participated in the siege of Tobruk, with little success against the British *Matilda* II tanks. The Ram division was more successful with its M tanks in the Bir el Gobi action against *Crusader* tanks of the British 22nd Armored Brigade, which had their own design problems.

In April 1941, when the *Afrika Korps* entered North Africa in force, the Italians still had 240 M13s and M14s in front-line service, but subsequent events proved that this tank was insufficiently armored.

▼ M13/40 tanks disembarked in Libya in large numbers at the beginning of the conflict. State Archives (author's colouring).

MEDIUM TANK M13-40 IN NORTH AFRICA

▲ M13/40 of 1st Platoon, 1st Company of VI Battalion of 132nd Ariete Armoured Division in the Libyan Desert March 1941.

▲ M13/40 tank in North Africa 1941. Bundesarchiv (author's colouring).

CARRO ARMATO MEDIO M13-40 IN AFRICA SETTENTRIONALE

▲ M13/40 Tank of the 132nd Ariete Armoured Division in the Libyan desert of Cyrenaica. Note the addition of tracks to reinforce the turret, an indication that this was a crew of African veterans. January 1942.

MEDIUM TANK M14-41 (CAPTURED) IN NORTH AFRICA

▲ M14/41 Italian tank captured by Australian troops in the North African campaigns. Subsequently framed in the 6th Australian cavalry Regiment. December 1941.

Many crews in an attempt to increase its defenses chose to pile sandbags on the vehicle's hulls, but this only contributed to further overheating the engine, reducing speed and increasing overall failures. This unnecessary practice, although popular, was discouraged by Italian commanders for the same reason. To try to cope with the disadvantage, the Royal Army equipped at least one company of each tank battalion with the more heavily armed Self-propelled 75/18.

Although they were still massively used during the first battle of El Alamein, by the time of the second battle in late 1942, the Allies began to deploy the new M3 Lee/Grant medium tanks and Crusader Mk IIIs, and then Shermans and together 6-pound (57 mm) towed anti-tank guns in their infantry units. It was then that the inherent weaknesses of the Italian medium became very evident. Losses increased significantly and the rest of the Littorio, Ariete and Centauro armored divisions, and later the Trieste Motorized Division, were almost totally destroyed during the retreat of the Axis troops to Tunisia and the ensuing campaign. Several vehicles were also retained in mainland Italy, participating in the Yugoslav campaign and later being used for anti-partisan actions. Twenty-two of these vehicles, especially M14, were eventually captured and reused after September 1943 by the Germans (detachments of the 2nd *SS SturmGeschütz* and *Panzerabteilung* Adria). The Second Battle of El Alamein saw the first appearance of the M4 Sherman, which proved as easy to imagine to be a real killer of the inferior armed and armoured Italian tank, despite the bravery of their crews. The retreat (as already mentioned) was a bloodbath. The Centaur Division was practically destroyed fighting in Tunisia. The M13/40 and M14/41 were now completely outgunned by the new Allied vehicles as were the Panzer III and IV of the Afrika Korps (were) to some extent and their armament was almost useless against the enemy's M3 Lee and M4 Sherman medium tanks, unless the enemy vehicles were only a few dozen meters away, while both Allied tanks could easily destroy an M13/40 from a distance. The Italian armored units resorted to defensive tactics by trying to fire at the suspensions and tracks and relying increasingly on the fire support of Self-propelled and field artillery.

▼ An M14/41 fording a river. (State Archives).

The first unit to receive the M14/41 tank was the 10th Battalion of the 133rd Armoured Division 'Littorio', which was later transferred to the Ariete Division Tank Infantry Regiment, followed by the IV, XII and LI Battalions of the 133rd Tank Infantry Regiment, also of the Littorio. It was also assigned to the 14th and 17th Battalions of the 31st Infantry tank Regiment of the Centauro; to the 15th of the 1st Infantry Division 'Superga'. These units and their tanks fought all the battles of the war in North Africa until the end, except for the 12th Battalion of the Littorio, which was sunk with all its M14/41s during the crossing of the Sicilian Channel, from the two battles of El Alamein, to the defence of the Mareth Line, from the victorious battle of Jebel bou Kournine against the British on 25 April 1943 with the *'Piscitelli'* Regiment, to the last armoured battle of the war in Africa on 8 May 1943. At home, these vehicles were assigned to the XVIII Battalion and the XVI Mixed Battalion, stationed in Sardinia. After the withdrawal of Italian forces from North Africa, the M14/41 largely disappeared, although many captured vehicles were put into service by British and Australian forces to fill the severe Allied tank shortage in 1941. However, these vehicles did not remain in Allied service for long. During the harsh battles, the flaws of this model became apparent. It was notoriously unreliable, cramped and caught fire easily when hit despite the diesel fuelled engine. Following the November armistice, while other models were captured and massively reused by the Germans, only one M14/41 was retained. Instead, the M14/41 was more widely used by the National Republican Army, especially for anti-partisan warfare. Some M14/41s reappeared in one of the last battles of the war, on 26 April 1945, when two of them plus two L40s of the RSI's 'Leonessa' unit, under the command of Lieutenant Arnold Rinetti, held American tanks in check for a good three hours at the gates of Piacenza.

▼ Two Italian tankers sitting on the hull of their M13/40 in North Africa in 1942 (State Archives).

MEDIUM TANK M13-40 IN TUNISIA

▲ M. 3/40 Tank of the 7th Battalion of the 132nd Ariete Armoured Division on the Mareth line. Tunisia, March 1943.

▲ Uniform of the Italian tank drivers 1940-1943. Artwork by the author.

■ OPERATING SPECIFICATIONS OF THE M15/42

The Regio Esercito, before collapsing in the aftermath of September 8th, had time to put eighty-two new M15/42 tanks into service, which it distributed to the cavalry and tank forces without forming large units, given the low production. The bulk of the vehicles went to the 135th Armoured Division 'Ariete': each of the three mixed groups making up the 10th Armoured Cavalry Regiment 'Lancieri di Vittorio Emanuele II', which was part of the division, was to have one squadron out of twenty-five M15/42s (the other two were equipped with 75/18 self-propelled vehicles) and the 10th Reserve Squadron out of ten tanks.

A few other formations were equipped with M15s: the 18th and 19th Battalions each had one company out of twenty tanks; the 10th Group, formed on 1 August 1943 to complete the staff of the 10th 'Lancieri di Vittorio Emanuele II' Regiment, only got twelve M15/42s; a further five vehicles converted into command wagons formed the Radio (Centre) Tank Platoon of the 135th Armoured Division.

Finally, an unknown number of vehicles remained in storage with the 33rd Tank Regiment.

The 135th Armoured Division used M15/42s during the terrible defence of Rome (8-10 September 1943), in countering the German invasion of Italy following the signing of the armistice, with very modest results and many losses. On the other hand, a discrete number of tanks were employed by the armed forces of the Italian Social Republic as well as by various German units in the last years of the war, both inside and outside the peninsula, often in anti-partisan combat. The 'Leonessa' Armoured Group had several M15s at its disposal. On the occasion of the visit that the Duce Benito Mussolini made to Milan towards the end of the war, he climbed onto the turret of the M15/42 under the command of Vice Brigadier Donati, lecturing the soldiers and civilian population gathered in front of the Muti barracks.

At the end of the Second World War, several M15/42s were reused by units of the newly formed Italian Army and State Police until the early 1950s.

■ IN THE 1948 ARAB-ISRAELI WAR

During the 1948 Arab-Israeli war, two or three M13/40s that remained in North Africa were incorporated into the Egyptian armed forces. These vehicles were used during the Negba battles, where one was disabled and later captured by Israeli troops. For some years after the war, the tank remained on the Negba kibbutz as a souvenir-monument to the battle.

■ CONCLUSIONS

The M13/40 had undeniably good characteristics, including relative ease of production, a sober diesel engine, and a cannon that was quite efficient for its time. It was capable of piercing 45mm armour at 500m, with an effective HE projectile and good secondary firepower. Until 1942, the M tank was capable of knocking out most British light and medium tanks, but was essentially defenceless against heavier British tanks such as the Matilda and Valentine. The bolted hull always proved to be a danger to the crew, and with every impact suffered the hull plates had a tendency to break. In addition, the mechanical parts and the engine itself proved unreliable in the long term. Speed was too low, especially considering the specific weight of the craft. This, combined with a simplistic construction, and numerous other inherent technical problems made it more vulnerable to artillery fire. For this reason, the M13/40 was considered obsolete by early 1942. However, many M13/40s survived the war.

▲ View of the Italian M14/41 medium tank from above. On the turret the painted white circle for air recognition by friendly aircraft is clearly visible. Right: a bronze or aluminium badge was placed at the top left on the front plate of armoured vehicles from April 1936 to August 1943.

MEDIUM TANK M14-41 AT EL ALAMEIN - EGYPT

▲ M_4/41 Tank 1 of the 3rd Platoon, 2nd Company of the 11th Battalion of the 132nd Ariete Armoured Division at El Alamein. July 1942.

▲ Australian soldiers examine an M14-41, possibly abandoned for lack of fuel. Libya 1942.

▼ Rear view of an M13/40 tank (note the absence of track guards). Libya 1941.

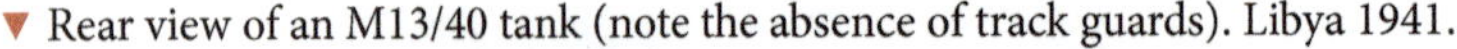

MEDIUM TANK M14-41 ON VIBERTI TRAILER, 1942.

▲ M14/41 Operating tank, loaded on Viberti trailer for transport. Italy or Balkans, 1942.

▲ View of the Italian M14/41 medium tank from the front and back.

▲ An M13/40 at a parade in Tripoli in front of the monument of the Duce on horseback with the sword of Islam.

COMMAND TANK M13-40, NORTH AFRICA 1942

▲ M14/41 Radio Command Tank 132nd Ariete Armoured Division, Libya 1942.

CAMOUFLAGE AND DISTINGUISHING MARKS

The background colours of the medium tanks, both M13-14-15 and M11, from their creation until 1945, (the operational period of this use is indicated in brackets) also used for all armoured vehicles were: R.E. grey green (1936-1945), dark chocolate (1936-1941), reddish brown (1936-1943), ochre (for prototypes), sand (1941-1945), dark sand (1943-1945), dark grey (1941-1943). For camouflage, medium green (1936-1943) and dark red (for prototypes) were used.

Medium tanks had not yet emerged at the time of the Ethiopian War 1935-1936 and the Spanish Civil War 1937-1939. *National territory 1936-1940* - substantial predominance of grey-green. Occupation of *Albania and French Front 1939-1940* - grey-green.

Campaign of Greece and Yugoslavia 1940-1941 - grey-green possibly camouflaged with green and sand-coloured flecks. *East Africa 1940-1941* - grey green or in the old Ethiopian campaign camouflage reddish brown with green spots. *North Africa 1940-1943* - at first only green-grey, the colour in which they were generally landed at destination ports, then sand-coloured in various variegated versions. Not used in the Russian Campaign 1941-1943.

France and Corsica 1942 - grey-green and sand with possible reddish-brown patches. *CSR 1943-1945* dark sand grey-green, reddish brown with medium dense green flecks, in uniform German panzer grey colour. In particular, the tanks of the Leonessa and partly also the Leoncello were dark sand in colour. Elaborate camouflage in irregular chequered patterns of sandy yellow background and green and brown patches.

MEDIUM TANK BADGES

In order to recognise individual armoured vehicles in military operations, even for Italy, it became necessary to introduce an identification system, also because, at least initially, there were no tanks with radios installed. In fact, radios only began to be installed with some regularity from 1941 onwards. In the beginning, flags with red or white drapes were used for communication.

The first table of distinctive tank markings dates back to 1925 and was very complex and articulated to excess. Number groups were only introduced in 1927 after the establishment of the Tank Regiment, and new regulations were issued in 1928. In 1940, the first deliveries of M13/40 Tanks finally began, which were distributed to the various armoured divisions.

The Medium tanks, as had already been the case with the Light tanks, bore symbols identified by markings, names and numbers placed on both sides of the hull. The numbers were painted on the front of the hull plate and on both sides.

In 1938, to simplify recognition, a further change was made, this time a radical one: new tactical tank symbols were established. This system was also followed by the medium tanks that came into being a few years later. The tank companies were represented by coloured rectangles as follows:

The first company had the colour red, the 2nd company blue, the 3rd company yellow, the 4th company green; the colour white was reserved for regimental command tanks. The insignia of the tanks and armoured cars had to be 20 x 12 cm in size and painted in the company colour.

The coloured rectangles were cut by white bars (1 to 4 lines and a diagonal for 5th platoon) and indicated the different platoons, full colour and without lines for Company Command tanks.

The rectangles of the various platoons were surmounted by an Arabic number (the colour of the company) indicating the tank in the platoon's organic formation.

These numbers had to be 10 cm high and 1.5 cm thick, and placed in the centre of the upper side of the rectangle 2 cm apart. Below the rectangle the number of the battalion to which it belonged was placed in white Roman numerals. Battalion tanks, if in reserve at Regimental level, instead bore only the relative

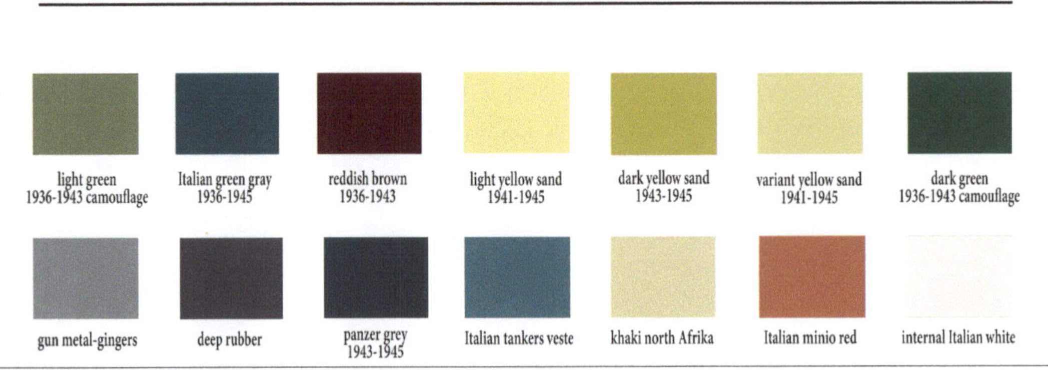

WW2 ITALIAN TANK &AFV COLORS & CAMOUFLAGE

Arabic number. Battalion command squadron tanks had a completely black rectangle. The battalion command tank on two companies had it half red and half blue on the right. The battalion command tank on three companies had it on three coloured lines from left to right: red, blue and yellow.

Specifically for the medium tanks, the distinctive sign was placed on the turret in the front mid-upper part. At the rear, in the middle part of the turret. On some tanks, the rectangle was placed at the height of the access hatch to the combat chamber. On the same hatch, the distinctive sign of the Division, such as a black ram, often appeared. As an aerial identification sign on the vehicles, a white Savoy cross was sometimes painted in the summer of 1940 and placed, depending on the type of vehicle, on the turret or engine compartment ceiling. From 1941, a white disc 70 cm in diameter was painted instead of the cross. Although the circular clearly stated, there were numerous exceptions and variations to the official regulations.

The medium tanks used by the Italian Social Republic showed the distinguishing marks of the various departments painted on them: the 'Leoncello' was depicted by a black lion clutching a fascio littorio looking to the left on a white background. The 'Leonessa' had a slightly more complicated distinguishing sign formed by the red M of Mussolini, cut by a black fasces and underneath the always black inscription 'GNR'.

Instead of the coloured rectangles, a rectangle of the same size was used with the simple tricolour flag or the republican type with a black eagle in the centre. The numbers both below and above were always white.

The tanks used by the Germans, especially the captured ones, and the new ones ordered after the armistice of 1943 bore the typical German army markings starting with the black and white *ritterkreuz* in its various forms.

▲ An Italian M14/41 tank with the tank leader in the turret in November 1940 on the Greek Albanian front.

MEDIUM TANK M15-42 - ITALY, MARCH 1943

▲ M15/42 Battalion command tank of the 32nd Tank Regiment in Sardinia in 1943.

▲▼ M13/40 tanks with their crews on the outside of the vehicle. Libyan Front 1940-1941.

MEDIUM TANK M15-42 - ITALY, MARCH 1943

▲ M15/42 of the 132nd Tank Regiment of the Ariete II Armoured Division in training in Friuli in the spring of 1943.

MEDIUM TANK M15-42 - LIBERATION OF ROME, SEPTEMBER 1943

▲ M15/42 of VII Squadron, 1st Platoon of Armoured Division "Ariete" at the defence of Rome, 8-10 September 1943.

PRODUCTION AND EXPORT

From the start of the war onwards, 710 M13/40, 730 M14/41 tanks (divided between tanks and command vehicles) and between 110 to 250 M 15/42 were built. This amounted to a total of about 1550/1700 vehicles in the different variants. Since production began during wartime, there were no international markets available to sell the vehicles, as was the case with the light tanks, for example. The tanks, especially due to wartime events, ended up in the hands of various belligerent and or allied and former allied nations.

- Royal Army, buyer and major user of most of the production of medium armoured vehicles.
- Australia. Following the battles in the North African desert, Australian troops took possession of a number of armoured vehicles, mainly M11/39, M13/40 and M14/41. These vehicles were rehabilitated by the Australians themselves and repainted with typical colours and markings (the famous white kangaroos).
- Great Britain: as above, British troops also got their hands on some Italian medium tanks.
- Italian Social Republic: after the collapse of Italy following the events of September 8, a new state was created in northern Italy controlled by the Germans. The RSI used all the military means already of the Royal Army at its disposal.
- German Army: In the same way and in a massive and selective manner, the German Army also confiscated and repurposed all Italian vehicles at its disposal after September 8. In some cases even reactivating the production assembly lines (especially in the case of M15 vehicles and self-propelled derivatives).

MAJOR USER

Medium tanks were used by the armies mentioned above, but obviously the main user was Italy and its armoured units: by the Regio Esercito above all, but also, after the Armistice, by the Esercito Nazionale Repubblicano and the Guardia Nazionale Repubblicana, following the establishment of the Italian Social Republic in 1943. A few vehicles were also captured in the European theatres of war, especially in Dalmatia and the Balkans, captured and reused by the Yugoslav partisans and the Greek resistance. Some of these vehicles remained in service in Italy for a short time during the immediate post-war years, as part of police operations. Finally, there is the singular case of a pair of tanks that remained in Egypt, probably captured by the British, and were left by them to the Egyptian army, which used them to fight the first Arab-Israeli war in 1948.

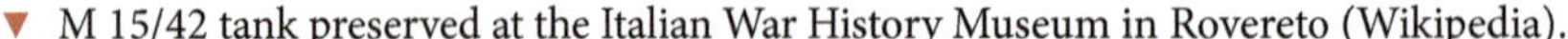

▲ M13/40 tanks massing in a desert depression. Libyan front 1940-1941. Small photo: an M13/40 on the Tunisian front shortly before the Axis troops abandoned Africa.

▼ M 15/42 tank preserved at the Italian War History Museum in Rovereto (Wikipedia).

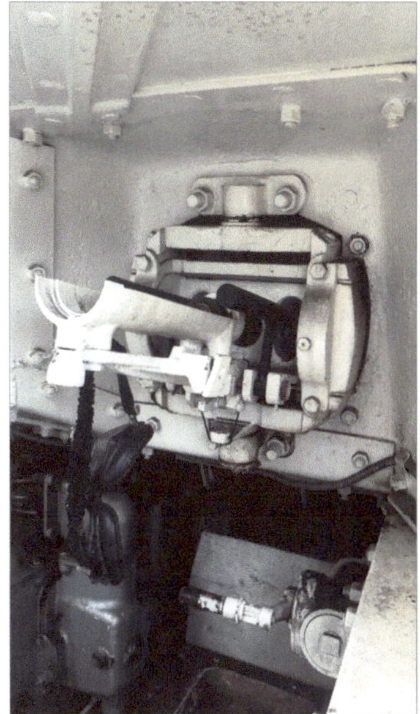

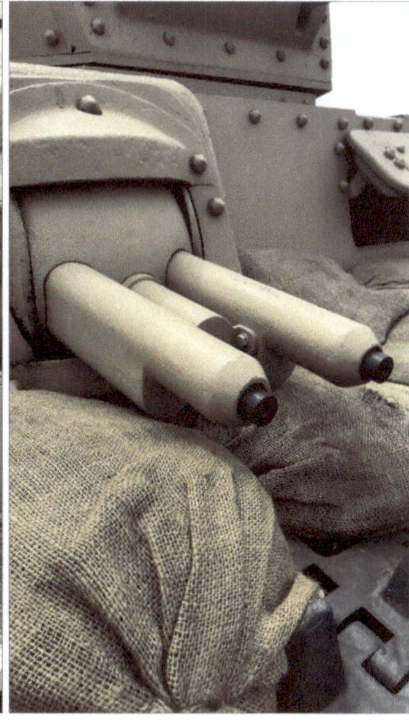
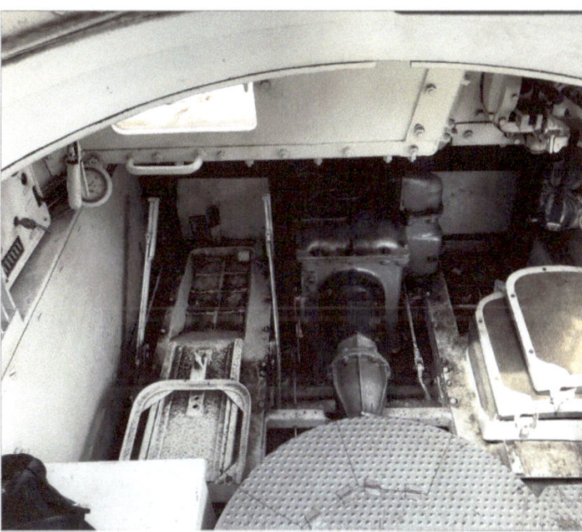

▲ Various details of the M15/42 tank exhibited at the Militaria fair in Novegro (MI). Photo by the author.

▲ Back of the M14/41 exhibited at the British Museum in Bovington. (Wikipedia).

▼ Another picture of General Mario Balotta next to some of his staff officers. Commander of the Ariete Division and winner of the Battle of Bir el Gobi. Libya 1941.

MEDIUM TANK M15-42, CROATIA 1944

▲ M15/42 Tank captured and put into use by the German Armed Forces, Croatia 1944.

	M13/40	M14/41	M15/42
Length	4915 mm	4915 mm	5060 mm
Width	2280 mm	2280 mm	2280 mm
Height	2270 mm	2370 mm	2370 mm
Minimum bottom-hull height from ground	0,38 m	0,38 m	0,41 m
Weight in combat order	14.000 kg	14.500 kg	15.000 kg
Crew	4	4	4
Engine	M 13: Fiat-SPA 8T M.40 8-cylinder V diesel, 11,140 cm³ M 14: Fiat SPA 15T M.41 diesel, 8-cylinder V-cylinder, 11980 cm³ M 15: FIAT-SPA 15TB M.42 8-cylinder V-cylinder, petrol-powered		
Maximum speed	30 km/h on road 15 km/h off road	32 km/h on road 16 km/h off road	40 km/h on road 20 km/h off road
Autonomy	210 km on road 5 h off road	200 km on road 5 h off road	220 km on road 5 h off road
Tank capacity	180 L	180 L	400 L
Armour thickness	From 6 to 42 mm	From 6 to 42 mm	From 6 to 42 mm
Armament	1 cannone 47/32 Mod. 1935 da 47 mm. 3 mitragliatrici Breda Mod. 38 da 8 mm	1 cannone da 47/32 Mod. 39. 3-4 x mitragliatrici Breda cal. 8 mm	1 cannone 47/40 Mod. 38 da 47 mm. 3 mitragliatrici Breda Mod. 38 da 8 mm

▼ Possible hypothetical variable of the German 'feldgrau' paint scheme of the M15 anti-aircraft on the opposite page.

MEDIUM ANTI-AIRCRAFT TANK M15-42, AUSTRIA 1944-45

▲ M15/42 Anti-Aircraft Prey Tank, captured by the Germans at Cecchignola in 1943 and then used until 1945 to fight the Soviet army in Austria.

▲ Huge storehouse of Italian armored vehicles, mainly medium and self-propelled tanks, which fell into German hands after the 1943 armistice.

▼ A "Germanized" M15/42. The Germans christened the new Italian tank Pz.Kpfw. 738

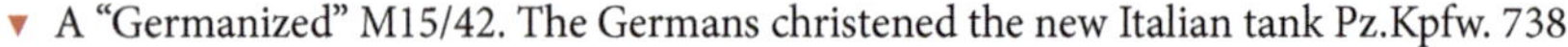

MEDIUM TANK M13-40, CIVIL WAR 1943-45

▲ M13/40 Anti-Partisan Regiment tank used during the Italian Civil War 1943-45.

MEDIUM TANK M13-40, CIVIL WAR 1943-45

▲ M13/40 Armoured Group 'Leonessa' tank used during the Italian Civil War 1943-45.

MEDIUM TANK M15-42, CIVIL WAR 1943-45

▲ M15/42 Armoured Group tank of the 'Leoncello' used during the Italian Civil War 1943-45.

BIBLIOGRAPHY

- *Carro M - carri medi M 11-39, M 13-40, M 14-41, M 15-42, semoventi e altri derivati*, Antonio Tallillo, Andrea Tallillo, Daniele Guglielmi, Gruppo Modellistico Trentino, 2010.
- *Veicoli da Combattimento dell'Esercito Italiano dal 1939 al 1945.* Falessi, Cesare; Pafi, Benedetto (1976). Intyrama books.
- *Italian Medium Tanks, 1939–45. New Vanguard 195.* Cappellano, F.; Battistelli, P. P. (2012). Oxford: Osprey Publishing.
- *Italian Armored Vehicles of World War Two.* Pignato, Nicola (2004).Squadron/Signal publications.
- *Storia dei mezzi corazzati.* Pignato, Nicola. Vol. II. Fratelli Fabbri Editori.
- *I reparti corazzati italiani nei Balcani*, Paolo Crippa e Carlo Cucut. Soldiershop 2019.
- *I reparti corazzati del R.E. E l'armistizio 1° Volume*, Paolo Crippa. Soldiershop 2021.
- *I reparti corazzati del R.E. E l'armistizio 2° Volume*, Paolo Crippa. Soldiershop 2021.
- *Il gruppo corazzato del Leoncello*, Paolo Crippa. Soldiershop 2021.
- *I mezzi blindo-corazzati italiani 1923-1943*, Nicola Pignato, Storia Militare, 2005.
- *Gli autoveicoli da combattimento dell'Esercito Italiano, Volume secondo (1940-1945)*, Stato Maggiore dell'Esercito, Ufficio Storico, Nicola Pignato e Filippo Cappellano, 2002.
- *Corazzati Italiani 1939-1945*, Nico Sgarlato, War Set n°10, 2006.
- *Mezzi dell'Esercito Italiano 1935-45*, Ugo Barlozzetti & Alberto Pirella, Editoriale Olimpia, 1986.
- *Corazzati e blindati italiani dalle origini allo scoppio della seconda guerra mondiale*, David Vannucci, Editrice Innocenti, 2003.
- *Articolo di* Cédric Mas, Batailles & Blindés n°13-14, 2006.
- *"L'Ariete a Bir-El Gobi". Storia Militare (in Italian).* Maraziti, Antonio (Gennaio 2005). Albertelli edizioni.
- *Italian Medium Tanks in Action*, Nicola Pignato, 2001.
- *Le fiamme rosse del 31° Reggimento Carristi*, Maurizio Parri, Soldiershop, 2021.
- *Il gruppo corazzato "San Giusto" dal Regio Esercito alla RSI 1934-1945*, Stefano Di Giusto, Laran Éditions, 2008.
- *I reparti corazzati della Repubblica Sociale Italiana 1943/1945*, Paolo Crippa, Marvia Edizioni, 2006.
- *...Come il diamante, I Carrisit italiani 1943-45*, Sergio Corbatti & Marco Nava, Laran Edizioni, 2008.
- *Italian Tank M13/40, Preliminary report n° 18.* Military college of Science November 1943.
- *Storia dell'Ansaldo 6. Dall'IRI alla guerra 1930-1945*, Gabriele De Rosa, Gius. Laterza & Figli, 1999.
- *Italian Medium Tanks M13 and M14* by Iron Coffins, Museum Ordnance Special Number 1994.

TITLES PUBLISHED OR IN WORKING

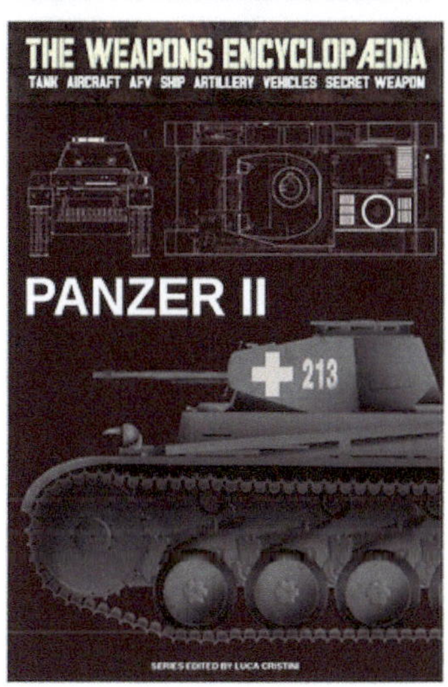

TWE-004 EN